# SHE TOO IS A SAILOR

**Antonia Jade King** is one of the hosts of Boomerang Club, and a previous Hammer & Tongue finalist. She was part of the Apples and Snakes Writing Room programme in 2018 and has performed at numerous events including Love Supreme festival and *Rallying Cry* at Battersea Arts Center. Antonia is studying for a master's researching the historical significance of black women in popular culture.

**She Too Is a Sailor**

Published by Bad Betty Press in 2019
www.badbettypress.com

Cover design by Amy Acre

Printed and bound in the United Kingdom

A CIP record of this book is available from the British Library.

ISBN: 978-1-9997147-8-9

Supported using public funding by the National Lottery through Arts Council England

# SHE TOO IS A SAILOR

ANTONIA JADE KING

PRESS

Okay ladies, now let's get in formation.

– Beyoncé Giselle Knowles-Carter

# She Too Is a Sailor

*For Mum*
*and the other women*
*who have saved me*

# Contents

# antonia jade king

In mum's mouth it means *I named you so men do not need to.*
In his mouth it sounds like mum's mistakes.
It sounds like *I will name you with my fist.*
It sounds like *I will name you ant,*
*ant* like small brown thing, something you do not want.
Occasionally I still hear him filling my name with ants.
Mum didn't name me before I was born,
unable to know me before she heard me cry,
he felt the same. She gave me her surname,
not a man's, thought that if they followed my name
maybe they'd follow me too but my name
is not protection from men or their fists.
I want a new name that only my mother knows
because this one now sounds like *ant,*
*ant* like small brown thing, *ant* like
*do you know how much she can hold on her back?*
I will give this name only to my mother,
it will not fall into the mouths of men
who still think me in need of naming.

i don't wanna outlive mum
sanitiser men say her recovery is good but
her face drops when she's tired
is it bad i can't see beauty in that?
i keep asking
if a memory can recover
or does it stay ill till it dies?
because the first face drop
is in my brain coughing
it has a metallic taste
how dare her brain do this to her
doesn't it know i need her
to outlive me

# six

She is six playing with barbies that don't look like her.
Her mum is behind her drinking tea or another hot drink
that does not interest six year olds. She turns to her mum and says
*I want two kids when I'm a grown up, both girls.*

Her mum gently reminds her of the doctor who had said the words
*slashed ovaries* and *it wouldn't happen naturally.*
She had wanted to ask how you could have a kid *unnaturally*
picturing robots or something like how unicorns give birth.

# maya and her protest are going furniture shopping

They have taught themselves how to sleep, they are collecting nice furniture and soft bed sheets because her body likes them,

giving soft melodies to audiences who ask for volume and power. Maya and her protest left a man because he didn't make them sing.

When Malcolm died they went to Harlem
to be a fire extinguisher to a burning town.

Maya and her protest know to allow themselves soft bed linen. They know how to march, how to leave and save men.

They do not worry about perfect grammar. Maya and her protest do not smile for photographs unless they are happy.

They are in a headwrap and hoop earrings,
looking side on into a camera as if to say

> *I know you won't capture me perfectly, so*
> *I am going to sleep now.*

## ten

I'm watching Will Smith
locked in a basement with his girlfriend,
she takes her wig off, there's an earthquake
he calls this wig deception, we laugh
he sings *girl getting on my nerves*
she throws her fake nails in his face, we laugh
he sings *I thought she was fine*
he calls her a liar, we laugh
he sings *don't know if her body is hers*
I'm ten questioning
what men will allow me to do to my face when I'm older

# if I know anything

*After Ocean Vuong*

I know that **the**
bite marks on my shoulder are the **best**
way to get you to talk to me and that the **way**
you show your love is simply **to**
cut things. I **understand**
you now, and in **a**
way is the best of a **man**
any more than bite marks and blood? **Is**
my fear of using my mouth **with**
force insulting to **your**
                    kind? I'll use my **teeth**

walking home you made me dance with you
to a busker singing lauryn hill

laugh so wide I exposed the back of my throat
we danced and the busker sang
*Girl you know you better watch out*
I did not hear her, I was laughing

# he breathes easily when

next to me He's smoking
eyes closed

playing music I like
like Bey and some old songs

in the hope I'll stop asking things
and sing instead

*ashes to ashes, dust to side chicks*

He hugs me from behind because
He breathes easier when not looking in my eyes

Bey is still singing about cheating men, I sing along
not asking

*girl, I can tell he's been pretending*

He hugs me from behind
breathes easily

# he had a girlfriend of five years

he was attractive in the same way as most men who make me feel
bad
white teeth made me want to be funny so he'd laugh or
do something else with his mouth
I sat on his couch that smelt like expensive weed and cheap gin with
my legs crossed
he started playing with my hair and said *for fuck's sake* with a laugh
*agreed* I replied, with something like a laugh but more serious

I used her hairband to tie mine up
it was easy not to think about her
with something more serious than a laugh
we flattened onto the bed
to bang our heads against bricks and see
if the walls would fall

# that night I began yelling

the word pride at mirrors. Sometimes
I fear I haven't got rid of all
the venom he yelled into my body,
I feel it somewhere in my fingertips
or hair when I sit
on Devon buses. Or when boys
with blue eyes look at me
too long. I don't have many
childhood memories but I
remember how
my belief in antidotes
died.

# the carol for those dreading christmas

| | | |
|---|---|---|
| You go | downstairs for breakfast, forgetting | to take your |
| bonnet | off. Your aunt's question will start a | war. You walk |
| around | your own family dodging grenades. | Your cousins' |
| laughter | doesn't sound like home. You | question why |
| you are | not laughing with them. You walk, | inhale the |
| country | because in that house, air that fills | their lungs |
| easily | doesn't reach yours. Maybe they | were |
| given | gas masks. Your other aunt will | brag that |
| her eyes | are slightly more blue than the rest | of theirs. Do |
| blue eyes | see better? Your uncle apologises | for the last |
| time you | were all together, says he doesn't | use that |
| word, | it was the alcohol. You wonder if | your mum |
| has ever | used that word, how much alcohol | it would |
| take. You | turn your side of the sofa into | a trench |
| question | where they have drawn their battle | lines. |
| You go | to bed at 9pm saying you have | a headache |
| dream of | what a peace treaty would look like. | They don't |
| even know | they started a war. You remember | the soldiers |
| who | stopped fighting to play football at | Christmas |
| knowing | they were going to kill each other at | breakfast. |

# conversations with my mother about love

My mum asks me why I politicise love. I tell her that love without politics feels fragile. That I am always fearful of uncharted water, maybe this fear is because my father is a sailor. Maybe this fear is because mum wears her pain like a piece of clothing she does not wish to remove.

I tell mum I have learnt not to use another human being as my anchor. Maybe I learnt this because my father is a sailor, but a terrible anchor. I have never been good at staying grounded so maybe I am looking for an ocean, although I saw my mother drown in an ocean with a sailor.

I am small as mum so maybe I need a river. I tell her that calm waters and love make me nervous. Perhaps these nerves are because my father is a sailor who taught me that when you are not fighting a storm you should check the horizon and keep your sails up. Maybe these nerves are because my mum has been battling these storms and not him.

I tell her she wears her pain like a piece of clothing she does not wish to remove, she tells me that's because I have a habit of stealing her clothes. My mum told me men are sailors. She said *you will only ever be a boat to them. Use me as your anchor.* I tell her she looks too fragile to be an anchor, she smiles, and reminds me that she too is a sailor.

# there have been searchlights over croydon for two months

now not screaming means

blood or something similar

I noticed him two streets ago

now my steps have doubled

and I see the searchlights

I hear mum's grief

at my front door, two streets away

# the moon is a woman so how dare you do this in front of her

yelling about my boobs or ass or
something else I've had
since age twelve          I go home
and watch Bey
take over the louvre

# Acknowledgements

Thank you to everyone in the poetry scene who has allowed me to grow and witness them do the same. Also, thank you to Jake and Amy at Bad Betty Press for giving me this opportunity.

# Other titles by Bad Betty Press